Anger Management

How to Master Your Anger, Control Your Emotions And Find Joy In Life

Howard Patel

Anger Management

Written by Howard Patel

First Edition

Copyrights Notice

Limited Liability

Please note that the content of this book is based on personal experience and various information sources.

Although the author has made every effort to present accurate, up-to-date, reliable, and complete information in this book, they make no representations or warranties concerning the accuracy or completeness of the content of this book and specifically disclaim any implied warranties of merchantability or fitness for a particular purpose.

Your particular circumstances may not be suited to the example illustrated in this book; in fact, they likely will not be. You should use the information in this book at your own risk.

All trademarks, service marks, product names, and the characteristics of any names mentioned in this book are considered the property of their respective owners and are used only for reference. No endorsement is implied when we use one of these terms.

This book is only for personal use. Please note the information contained within this document is for educational and entertainment purposes only and no warranties of any kind are declared or implied. Readers acknowledge that the author is not engaged in providing any kind of medical, dietary, nutritional, psychological, psychiatric advice, nor professional medical advice.

Please consult a doctor, before attempting any techniques outlined in this book. Nothing in this book is intended to replace common sense or medical consultation or professional advice and is meant only to inform. By reading this book, the reader agrees that under no circumstances is the author responsible for any losses, direct or indirect, which are incurred as a result of the use of the information contained within this document, including, but not limited to, errors, omissions, or inaccuracies.

Table of Contents

Introduction

Anger is an expression of hostility in reaction to dissatisfaction. The dissatisfaction can stem from a variety of sources; a reaction to bad news you received, something that was done to you or you perceive was done to you, an argument you had, or even just your perception of things and people in your life; even depending on your mood to start with, something as quick as another driver cutting you off, or a cashier giving you back the wrong change can trigger anger.

We've all gotten angry over large and small issues, and overreacted to bad news or something annoying. The expression of anger becomes an issue when we cross the line from a simple expression of dissatisfaction to a consistent overreaction that harms ourselves and people around us emotionally, psychologically, or even physically.

Can Anger Be Appropriate?

Yes. Anger is one way of expressing that you don't like how you've been treated, letting another person know, I want this fixed and made right, or you're upset about something.

Expressing anger lets someone know, this is somewhat serious, at least to me. This needs attention and resolution if possible.

People would be surprised if you didn't get angry over some things. Anger is a normal emotion and part of every day with its purpose and proper time.

You could get angry over losing your job, if someone stole something from you, if your car broke down, when a partner breaks up with you, arguing with a family member when you feel like someone's not giving you enough respect, or your fair due. These are just a few examples of when people would expect you to get angry and you'd have a right to. Various causes and reasons can trigger anger. It happens to us all. It's perfectly normal, up to a point, and within moderation.

Sometimes you need to express anger before you can begin to resolve an issue, especially if it involves someone else who thus far hasn't considered your side of the issue.

Can You Use Anger Constructively?

Anger expresses dissatisfaction. You can use anger constructively to make your feelings clear and express a need to resolve an issue.

If someone cuts you in line at the coffee shop every morning, you can get angry, letting them know you don't like being cut. They might acknowledge it and back off the following morning and let you go first. You've expressed your dissatisfaction and resolved the conflict.

You feel like your parents never listen to you. You might get angry during a discussion or argument. They might wonder why you're so angry and ask why.

Then you can explain your feelings, you feel like they never listen to you. It hurts your feelings and your self-esteem. Who hasn't blurted something out in a heated family argument?

As long as it's not an intentionally insulting, hurtful comment, "you're stupid", "you don't care", then you're expressing your feelings toward resolving a conflict. Your parents will make more of an effort to listen the next time you argue.

Anger can be used to define boundaries. The person at the coffee shop knows you don't like being cut.

You could get angry if someone slaps you on the back unexpectedly. They'll know you don't like that and hopefully won't do it again.

Some people get angry when you talk to them while they're reading. Some people get angry if you sit too close to them.

They're expressing a need for boundaries, as long as they're not insulting or hurtful.

You can use anger constructively to express concern over how someone is treating you.

If you shout, "get off my back," while someone's asking you for something, you're expressing anxiety, telling them, please, not right now. You might be too brief, and hopefully, later you'll make time to discuss it further, calmly and politely, but you've expressed concern or stated a need through anger.

Anger can be a constructive way to simply vent, or cathartic, blow off steam, provided you're not mistreating someone in the process. You might kick a rock when you're tired from gardening. You might stamp your mouse if your computer freezes.

Provided you don't break something or hurt someone, we all need to blow off steam sometimes.

You should consider whether you have an anger control issue if you break things regularly, or if you hurt someone's feelings, or even hurt someone physically.

Like you can express boundaries through anger, you can express preferences in behavior or routines. "Do you have to do that now?", "Why is it always after lunchtime?" are expressions of anger that let someone know you'd prefer they did or said something at a different time, find a new routine you're both happy with. Again, discuss it more when you're calm.

Angry commands can become a form of control and abuse. Anger can be used constructively for various purposes if it's not taken too far or used too often.

How Can Anger Control You?

Anger can control you in a variety of ways, psychologically, emotionally, even physically, and can control how you handle people or situations, even how little problems escalate into big problems.

You can get so angry that all you think about is how to retaliate for a perceived wrong. You're in a psychological frame of mind to do damage and seek payback or revenge, not resolve a conflict for both parties' sake.

After a few bad fights with someone, you might decide you just can't get along with that person. Your anger has made you decide it is pointless to try. That's one more bridge you've burned because you couldn't work through your anger to repair the relationship.

Too many angry fits and your personality may begin to change. You might start to become an "angry person", quick to anger, upset more often than not.

Your total outlook might change for the worse. You might become pessimistic or cynical when previously you were usually hopeful and optimistic. Once you're becoming pessimistic, you'll behave differently. When previously you might try something new, now you might think, why bother, or, I'm bound to fail, so why try at all?

As you might adopt a negative attitude about new things and situations, you might adopt negative attitudes about people too, new people you meet, and even people you already know. Why should I ask my wife to go out? She'll only say no.

Why bother asking my son to play basketball? He's only going to beat me again. When your outlook about people becomes negative, then how you treat them will change too.

You could find yourself being more critical of your wife or your son or whoever you're developing new negative attitudes about.

As your perspective about the person or situation changes, so can the way you deal with him or them. You might have made the best of it before. Now you think, what's the point? Whatever happens, happens.

You can begin to approach everything with a negative perspective, assume the worst from the start, and assume there's no point trying to improve something, a situation, a relationship.

People around you will begin to feed off or react to your negative perspective. They might talk to you less. They might try less to work things out with you. They might fight more often with you.

You can begin a downward spiral that gets worse and worse until anger and a negative outlook can turn into depression and feelings of hopelessness. You might lose touch with people who used to be close to you. As you stop trying, they stop trying, until one day they decide there's no point knowing you at all.

Chapter 1

Understanding of Anger

Anger may be completely ugly. With the misery and suffering it causes, you will have firsthand experience. Its poisonous impacts have been minimized in many aspects of life. Anger will wreck connections. This will raise the likelihood of heart problems. And it is just plain uncomfortable to have a life filled with anger.

You might not be confident that when you're mad, you should change the way you behave. But we agree you will, and we thank you for having picked up this book and explored the role of anger in your life. This is a huge step in leading a life that is more peaceful and prosperous.

When they're upset, it's very normal for people to respond strongly. People of all genders, levels of schooling, racial origins, and types of income do it.

We offer tales of individuals that have suffered from frustration in a wide variety of circumstances in this novel. All the stories have in common is that anger has gotten in the way of the desire to deal with the problems of life successfully.

This chapter aims to answer some simple anger questions, include reliable statistics, and present an information base that you can build on when you move forward with your goal of changing your actions while you are angry.

We will help you make sense of the many components of anger, and we are going to answer common questions about it. And you will have to ask yourself this simple question at some point: "Is my anger helpful?"

Anger can be hard to grasp. In reality, you may have both felt satisfied and sad after the frustration you shared. You will possibly remember several occasions, for instance, when your frustration seems warranted, almost right.

"If you're like other people, you may have said to yourself," I'm entitled to be furious at what she did! "Nevertheless, if you are honest with yourself, you can accept that there have been times when your frustration was too intense, too long, needless issues created, or just plain foolish.

You could remember occasions when your irritation leads to fights, headaches, regrets, foolish actions, and other concerns, including when you felt it was acceptable.

One of our fundamental emotions is frustration. Scholars have written about frustration in people of all ages, and from all parts of the globe.

Some aspects of dissatisfaction are optimistic. It's part of relationships' ups and downs and can be a positive indication that something isn't right.

Any anger may also increase empathy between individuals. Your voice raised in anger, for instance, will indicate to people that you are talking about something important, and it will cause them to listen to you more closely.

Or anger will encourage you to make progress in your life and even face challenges that you've been avoiding. Zest, enthusiasm, and passion may also result from frustration.

The plain truth is that in a world without anger, we wouldn't want to exist. It has its advantages, and so this book isn't about removing anger from your life altogether.

But frustration can lead to severe damage and suffering as well. A typical effect of frustration is a disruption to ties with family members, acquaintances, and co-workers.

Angry people don't think straight, and the wrong choices are made. Furthermore, long-term frustration, such as heart disease and stroke, may cause significant medical complications. There are just a couple of the reasons for holding your frustration in place. If you read on, we'll send you some.

Anger is an intense reaction you are knowingly having. Anger is an internal perception of arousal at its heart, followed by individual emotions, perceptions, and desires.

What Causes Anger?

There are, in fact, many different triggers of anger. This is why, on TV, in newspapers, on the radio, and on the internet, you see experts sharing such different viewpoints. Let's start with an interpretation that brings together what most practitioners who research and treat anger accept:

Anger is an irrational response to others' unwelcome and sometimes unforeseen behavior. It arises based on the potential danger to physical wellbeing, possessions, personal appearance, sense of equality, or rational comfort wish.

How people portray frustration depends on where they are and whether it has worked for them in the past to communicate frustration.

First of all, this very formal definition applies to what we term an immediate cause: something negative happens (such as finding that a friend has been gossiping about you), and you react instantly with indignation.

You fault the other person for the way you behave when you're upset. This is considered a stimulus to reaction sequence by psychologists. The stimulation is the gossiping of your friend about you; your indignation is the answer. We will discuss some causes of anger;

- Learning
- Thinking
- Human nature

Learning

A lot of the irritation stems from patterns you've built over the years. Although there's always an instant trigger that gets you rolling, you've spent a long time learning when and how to get mad.

Sometimes, learning requires what psychologists call simulation. This suggests learning by watching what happens (in other words, learning by example) to other people as they get upset.

People tend to mimic others' actions, especially when they assume that specific actions create good outcomes. To list only a few examples, learning through modeling will come by watching the angry action of friends, colleagues, or characters on TV, in movies, and in video games.

In this way, there are a lot of ways to think about frustration. Then you take what you've heard about anger to turn it into your laws, such as, "When people insult me or gossip about me, I'm going to get mad to scream." That is me, and I do that! Not all angry behavior, of course, comes from watching people.

You have your distinctive, unique impressions and tradition of learning. Your history of learning consists of two sections, which are considered reinforcement and punishment by psychologists.

Although you usually don't think anything about it, repercussions accompany any of your actions. You prefer to replicate conduct that results in an outcome you like.

For starters, if you scream at your son to clean his room and he does it, the next time you ask him to clean his room, you are more likely to call at him again. Conduct that is enhanced (yelling at your son) in the short term becomes a long-term habit.

In comparison, the action is often accompanied by a result that you don't like. For starters, if you aggressively demand strangers to be quiet in a movie theatre, then they swear at you, a reaction that leads to a loud, then unpleasant argument, you are less likely to tell strangers to be quiet in the future.

Conduct that is punished in the short term should not become a habit (telling strangers to be quiet). Reinforcements and punishments powerfully form your patterns over time.

When you're mad, the way you behave now has a lot to do with the repercussions of your past mad conduct.

Thinking

Anyways of thought trigger frustration as well. You can misunderstand or misrepresent what other individuals do or say, for instance. You may be exaggerating, turning small issues into significant deals.

Or your opinions can be challenging and inflexible. You probably believe the following suggestions when angry:

- You've been forgotten, overlooked, or poorly punished.
- Somebody else has behaved incorrectly.
- If he/she had wanted to, the person who angered you might have behaved differently.
- The person who offended you ought to have behaved better.

Your assumptions about others' actions may or may not be valid.

There may be times where you have been wrong about other people's motivations. Perhaps the friend who is not answering your calls or responding to your messages struggles with personal or family member health issues. Job assignments can be overwhelmed by the future deadline that keeps holding you off.

Or maybe it was late for your teenage daughter, who is expected to be home by dinner time when she stopped at the mall to get you a birthday present. She wouldn't want to tell you that and spoil the surprise.

You don't actively analyze your thinking about poor treatment at others' hands, whether you're like most individuals. It only seems that your feelings arrive naturally.

However, unfortunately, the assumptions will become skewed, unreliable, and inflated over time. It is your thought, in that sense, which triggers your anger.

We'll return to this theory and teach you how to analyze and alter the exaggerated and skewed pieces of your mind.

Human Nature

Anger turned out to be part of human nature. In nonhuman species, anger may still occur, and the reasons for angry and violent actions in other species are equivalent to our motives for such activities.

For instance, monkeys display anger when they threaten their territories and when other monkeys attempt to take their food or mate with their partners. When they're mad, other animals do stuff to make themselves look large and stable.

These behaviors include making their bodies appear larger, standing, hissing, growling, biting, kicking, and scraping on their hind legs. Such activity is like a lot of our own. It is a warning to stay away as animals growl or hiss.

Our yelling sounds much like their growling. When animals stand straight and get larger, they say they're too powerful to mess with. That's equivalent to waving a hand in a provocative stance or bending forward.

When we feel challenged, anger comes out, and it worked with ancient humans. Around the same time, just an inclination or an impulse to behave with frustration is implicated with our resemblance to other species.

We can conquer these impulses as individuals who are often influenced by thought, affirmation, communities, classes, and community.

What is Aggression?

There is always a misunderstanding between anger and its cousin, hostility. Anger is an emotion that you experience mainly inside. Aggression is a behavior that may be witnessed by anyone.

Usually, violent conduct towards other people is seen, which involves throwing objects, pushing, shoving, punching, etc. Sneaky, indirect acts, such as scraping someone's car or removing office equipment from a co-worker you do not like, are also included.

Offensive conduct varies from comparatively mild to extreme (assault and murder) (a teen who throws a school mate in frustration). When we say that specific violence is minor, we don't intend to display that identifying and analyzing it is unnecessary.

Intentionally offensive actions aimed towards another person is almost always inappropriate. Nonetheless, multiple violent acts can have various harmful effects. In contrast to being struck in the chest, being hit by a hurled pencil at school is minor.

Aggression often entails the intent factor. The conduct may have been purposely carried out for you to classify the behavior of your partner, wife, or child (or of an acquaintance, stranger, or co-worker) as hostile.

Usually, we should not perceive dentists or physical therapists as aggressive, even if any acute discomfort can be induced. The statute treats intentional and accidental offenses as somewhat distinct.

Deliberate violence is treated even more harshly than accidental violence, like where an individual is injured in an automobile crash, like where crime is anticipated.

Likewise, a friend's deliberate bad conduct is much more important than his or her unintended behavior. You'd be smart to determine whether or not their acts were intentional if you're questioning the adverse conduct of people in your life.

Does Anger Cause Aggression?

The fuel for violence is often anger. However, most frequently, anger arises without provocation. And violent actions often occur without frustration. For instance, hunters are aggressive-their aim to kill animals, but they do not harbor resentment towards those animals.

Aggression with Anger

You may think anger and violence are like conjoined twins if you read the papers. An angered man beats his mother after an argument; an angry employee threatens a boss after not getting a rise, an angry youth shoots his teachers or friends after he is ignored or mistaken. You also hear about passion crimes.

Yet the real picture of the relationship between anger and violence is blurred by these high-profile events.

Some people indeed have good associations between their frustration, and aggression-they believe it's OK to be offensive when they're mad.

And a lot of the abuse that we witness and read about on the television is due to anger, which makes anger and provocation seem like they all happen together.

But really, it is the case, not the norm. The reality is, less than 10 percent of the time, deliberate physical violence accompanies frustration. Anger happens on its own most of the time, and it's anger itself that is the right challenge for most people.

This suggests that anger reveals itself only as shouting, complaining, verbally demeaning, frowning, being in a bad mood, or pouting, 90 percent of the time, not as violence.

Especially if one person assaults another (an upset adult, for instance, says, "I'm going to let you have it!"), violence normally does not accompany anger.

By this, we say that there are no physical acts associated with shouting and complaining that are measurable. Nevertheless, the value of the relationship between anger and violence we don't want to downplay.

Aggression is often accompanied by anger, as when the arousal and physical excitement of anger is accompanied by feelings of retaliation and malicious behavior.

Nevertheless, regardless of whether it is accompanied by violence, anger is a significant issue in its own right.

Aggression without Anger

Without anger, violence, and damage to other humans may also happen. For starters, in one case, a New York teenager thoughtlessly dropped a frozen turkey into a passing car from a highway overpass, and a driver was seriously injured.

But the teen wasn't upset at the driver. He had no idea that his thoughtless behavior could have harmed anyone. Or occasionally, not out of anger, adolescents and adults act violently as part of a scheme to rob from others.

A purse snatcher can hurt the victim's arm and, during the robbery, throw her to the ground. The attacker is not furious at the survivor.

The aim is clearly to get her purse stolen.

Check If Your Anger is Normal?

You may question if your anger pattern is natural. One way to address this question is to ask whether, when you get upset, things in your life usually change or get worse.

The other way of handling this question is to understand your anger's frequency, severity, and length.

- **How much do you get angry?** In a survey we took of adults living in the city, we found that about 25 percent of individuals were angry one or two days per week. Almost every day, some of our study subjects mentioned feeling upset. A variety of issues, such as poor self-image, loneliness, shame, weaker relationships with friends and family members, headaches and other medical problems, and legal troubles, tended to go along with being angry. Another 25 percent of our test subjects indicated that they seldom, if ever, became upset. With far fewer family, medical, and legal concerns, these individuals tended to have far happier lives.

- **How intense is your anger?** A mild to moderate strength of feeling is included in the frustration we call natural. The more severe your irritation is, the more likely it is for you to create problems. Mild and Mild in the lives of most people, frustration does not cause significant damage to Individuals.

- **How long would the indignation last?** Some persons waste days, weeks, or months at others' mercy, focusing on past unfairness and crappy care. For long times, being angry interferes with getting on with life and with feeling pleasure and satisfaction.

Think of any of the moments when you've been nuts. Have you been wondering about it? Whether your anger was too weak, too intense, or was it, just right? Does the discontent arise too often?

Will it last long enough? While sometimes anger can be a Yeah, you have to closely examine your life to determine whether it's helping or hurting you.

If Men Get Angrier Than Women

Differences between men and women have to do with another common issue. Some people think that men are angrier and more volatile than women are.

Anger, though, tends to be an experience of equal opportunities, because the fact is that men and women are much more similar than they are different.

A few psychologists have also noticed that, more often than men, women get angry. From a large-scale study of experimental findings, for example, John Archer suggests that women are marginally more likely to get angry and use physical violence than men.

Of course, as men are usually heavier, they inflict more harm when they attack women. In our personal experience, both men and women have a lot of resentment.

For the same reasons, both sexes tend to get angry with almost equal frequency, and they perceive and articulate themselves in standard ways. So, you're certainly not alone, whether you're a woman or a man.

Chapter 2

Anger Management

Anger management aims to minimize the psychological arousal and emotions caused by anger. A person can't avoid or rid him or herself of the people or things that cause him or her to get angry, nor can he or she change them; however, he or she can learn to control his or her reactions.

Certain psychological tests are used to measure the strength or intensity of feeling of anger, how prone to anger an individual is, and how efficiently he or she can handle it.

However, the chances are good that if a person does have a problem in controlling anger, he or she is aware of it. People who tend to act out in ways that seem frightening or out of control often need help finding healthy ways of dealing with their emotions.

Most psychologists who specialize in anger management believe that some individuals are more prone to anger than others are. They are more hotheaded and get angry more intensely and easily than the average person does.

There are also certain types of individuals who do not exhibit anger in spectacular ways but are perpetually grumpy and irritable.

People who get angry easily do not always throw stuff, shout, and a curse. Sometimes, they sulk, withdraw into themselves, or fall physically ill.

Easily angered individuals have a low tolerance for frustration, according to psychologists, which means that they believe they should not have to face annoyance, inconvenience, or frustration. They find it difficult to take situations in stride and are extremely frustrated when situations seem somewhat unjust.

Most people believe anger to be a negative quality because they learn that it is okay to express any other emotion apart from anger.

Consequently, they do not learn how to manage it or channel it into a more positive and constructive outcome. Family background also plays a role when it comes to managing anger.

Usually, people who are quick to anger come from families that are not skilled at emotional expression, as well as chaotic and disruptive families.

It is never healthy or helpful to let it all hang out. Some individuals may use this as an excuse to hurt others. Acting out in anger usually escalates the aggression and anger and does nothing to help the person who is angry or the person he or she is angry with to deal with the problem. It is better to find ways of managing the anger by identifying what triggered it in the first place and then coming up with strategies to keep those triggers from pushing one over the edge.

Anger management involves a wide range of strategies and skills that can help with identifying the signs and symptoms of anger and handling triggers healthily and constructively. This process requires individuals to recognize anger at an early stage and to communicate their feelings and needs while remaining in control and calm. It does not involve avoiding associated feelings or holding in the feelings of anger.

Anger management is an acquired skill, which means that anyone can master this critical skill with time, dedication, and patience, and the payoff is great. Learning to manage and control anger and to express it appropriately and healthily can help people achieve their goals, build more solid relationships, and lead more satisfying and happy lives.

Whenever anger is negatively influencing a relationship or is leading to dangerous behavior, an individual may benefit from professional help, such as joining an anger management class or seeing a mental health professional. However, there are early interventions people can try. Many people find that they can effectively deal with their anger issues without resorting to professional help.

People may also choose to use counseling to control and manage their out-of-control anger, especially if it is negatively affecting their relationships and other important aspects of their lives. Licensed mental health professionals can help them find and develop a variety of effective techniques for changing their behavior and way of thinking to manage their anger better.

However, people with anger issues need to be honest with themselves and their therapist about their problem and ask about his or her approach to anger management. The approach should not be only about putting them in touch with their feelings and expressing them; rather, it should be about their precise anger problem. According to psychologists, by using professional help, a highly angry individual can move closer to a middle-range in about two to three months, depending on the technique used and the circumstances.

People with anger management issues indeed need to learn how to be more assertive, instead of becoming aggressive. However, individuals who do not feel or express enough anger should be the most avid readers of most courses and books on improving assertiveness. These individuals are more acquiescent and passive than the average person and tend to allow others to walk all over them. This is not the typical behavior of a highly angry person. Nevertheless, these books can contain some helpful techniques to employ in frustrating situations to manage anger.

Life is full of unpredictable events, loss, pain, and frustration. No one can change that; however, people can change the way they let such factors affect them. Anger management techniques can keep highly angry individuals from making angry responses that can make them unhappy in the end.

Anger Management Skills you need to have

Failure to manage one's anger often leads to a wide variety of problems, such as yelling at one's kids, health problems, saying stuff one will later regret, sending rude texts and emails, threatening one's workmates, or physical violence. However, anger management difficulties do not always have to be that serious. Nevertheless, people might just find that they waste tons of time and mental energy venting about things or people they dislike or thinking about situations that upset them.

Having anger management skills does not mean that one never gets angry. Rather, it is about learning how to identify, deal with, and express one's anger in productive and healthy ways. Everyone can learn these skills, and there is always room for improvement. Anger can range from mild irritation to full-blown rage. When left unchecked, these feelings can lead to aggressive behavior like damaging property, yelling at someone, or physically attacking someone. They may also cause people to withdraw from society and turn their anger inward.

Angry emotions turn into a serious problem when they are felt too intensely and too often, or when an individual expresses them in inappropriate and unhealthy ways. Anger management skills are meant to help people discover and use healthy strategies to express and reduce their angry feelings. Keeping one's temper in check can be quite difficult; fortunately, using a few simple anger management tips can help one to stay in control.

Cognitive Behavioral Skills

Research consistently proves that these skills are effective for improving anger management. They involve changing how a person thinks and behaves based on the notion that people's feelings, thoughts, and behaviors are all related or connected. A person's thoughts and actions or behaviors can either increase or reduce their emotions. Therefore, if people want to shift their emotional state away from feelings of anger, they need to change what they are doing and thinking about.

Cognitive-behavioral interventions for anger management involve turning away from the behaviors and thoughts that fuel one's anger. The flame of anger will not continue to burn without this fuel, which means that it will begin to die down, and one will calm down. The best strategy is to come up with a workable Anger Management and Control Plan, which will enable one to determine what to do when one starts losing cool.

Some of the most effective anger management tips include:

1.Identify the Triggers

People who have fallen into the habit of losing their cool should find it helpful to consider the things that trigger their anger, for example, fatigue, traffic jams, snarky comments, long queues, a stressful job, or other things that tend to shorten their fuse. This is not to say that they should start blaming other people or situations for their inability to keep their temper. Instead, understanding these triggers can help them plan accordingly.

They might choose to plan their day in a different way to help them manage their stress levels better. They might also employ some anger management strategies whenever they are about to encounter situations that they usually find frustrating to lengthen their fuse, which will minimize the risk of a single distressing situation, setting them off.

2.Determine Whether one's Anger is Productive or Disruptive

Before reacting to a stressful situation, people need to try to calm themselves down and ask themselves whether their anger is productive or disruptive. For example, if an individual is witnessing the violation of another person's rights, his or her anger might help find the courage to challenge the situation and changing it.

On the other hand, if a person's anger is threatening to force someone to lash out or is causing some form of distress, it may be disruptive. Therefore, it makes sense to find effective ways of changing an individual's emotions by staying calm.

3.Identify the Warning Signs

It often seems like anger overwhelms people in the blink of an eye. However, this is not the case, as there are always warning signs when one's anger is beginning to rise. It is important to recognize these signs to help one take appropriate action to rein it in and prevent it from erupting. Some of the physical warning signs of anger include clenching one's fists, increased heartbeat, or one's face feeling hot. One may also notice some cognitive changes, such as beginning to see red or feeling one's mind racing.

When people notice these warning signs, they have a good opportunity to make immediate interventions to prevent their anger from boiling over to a point where they might end up creating more and worse problems in their lives.

4.Think Before Speaking

During a heated moment, it is easy to say something stinging that one will later regret. Therefore, it is always better to take a few moments to breathe and collect one's thoughts before speaking, which will allow the other person or people involved in the situation to do likewise. Trying to stick it out or win an argument in a heated situation will only fuel one's anger. It is even better to walk away if the situation looks like it might become explosive, after explaining that one is not trying to dodge the subject. One can rejoin the discussion when one is feeling more composed.

5.Be Assertive and Express one's Anger

As soon as one is feeling calmer and thinking more clearly, one should express one's frustration in a non-confrontational but assertive manner. It is important to express one's needs and concerns directly and clearly without offending the other person or trying to control him or her.

6.Talk to a Trusted Friend

People who are experiencing feelings of anger should talk to someone who has a calming effect on them. Expressing their feelings or talking through a problem with that person may be very helpful. However, it is important to understand that venting can backfire in certain situations. For example, talking about all the reasons they dislike someone or complaining about their boss may add fuel to the flame of anger.

It is a common myth that venting makes people feel better. It can accomplish the opposite. Therefore, it is important to use this coping method with a high level of caution. A good plan of action if one is going to talk to a friend would be to work on finding a solution, not just vent. Talking with a friend about anything else other than the frustrating situation might work better.

7.Get Some Exercise

Anger tends to give people a surge of energy, which needs a productive outlet. The best way to put it to good use is to engage in exercise. Hitting the gym or going for a brisk walk will burn off the extra energy and tension. Also, engaging in regular exercise helps people decompress. Aerobic workouts, in particular, help to reduce stress, which helps improve people's tolerance levels.

8.Think in a Different Way

When people are angry, having angry thoughts tend to build up anger. Having thoughts like, "I cannot stand this traffic jam anymore," will exacerbate a person's frustration further.

Therefore, when people find themselves having thoughts that fuel their anger, they should reframe them and remind themselves of the real facts, such as there are millions of vehicles on the road every day, so there are bound to be traffic jams.

Focusing on the larger picture without adding distorted facts or frustrating predictions will help people stay calmer. It might also be helpful to develop a mantra that one can repeat to drown out negative thoughts that fuel anger, for example, saying, "I am ok and things will be fine," over and over again will help keep the thoughts that fuel one's rage at bay.

9.Find Possible Solutions

Instead of focusing on the things that made them angry, people should instead work on resolving the problem at hand. For example, if a child's messy room is driving him or her parent insane, solving the problem might be as simple as closing the door. People should always remind themselves that anger rarely solves anything, and it might make the situation worse.

10.Avoid Placing Blame

A tendency to always place blame or criticize might increase tension. A good way to avoid doing this is to stick with 'I' statements when describing a frustrating situation while being specific and respectful at the same time. For example, it is better to say, "I am upset because you came late" instead of saying, "you never come on time."

11.Avoid Holding Grudges

Forgiveness is a powerful and effective tool for managing anger. When people allow negative feelings to drown out positive ones, they end up finding themselves overcome by their sense of injustice or bitterness. However, when they choose to forgive people who have angered them, they might both end up learning from their experience and strengthen their relationship.

12.Release Tension Using Humor

A little humor can diffuse tension and lighten up the dark mood. Although it is difficult to do, people who are begging to feel angry should use humor to help them face whatever is upsetting them, or even any unrealistic hopes they may have for how things should go. That said they should take care not to use sarcasm, which can make the situation worse and hurt the other person's feelings.

13.Engage in Relaxation Techniques

There are tons of relaxation techniques to choose from, and people should find a few that work best for them. Progressive muscle relaxation and breathing exercises are two of the most effective exercises for reducing tension. Better yet, someone who is feeling frustrated and angry can perform both discreetly and quickly at any time.

14.Determine the Best Time to Seek Help

Learning to manage anger is a challenge for everyone sometimes. People who think their anger has gotten out of control and is causing them to do things they never thought they could ever do should seek professional help for their problem.

15.Use a Calm Down Kit

People who tend to take out their anger on their loved ones when they come home from work stressed out should create a kit to help them calm down and relax. It can be an object that helps engage their senses, such as a portrait of a beautiful and peaceful landscape, or an inspirational or spiritual passage about staying calm.

One of the most important lessons here is that it is possible to manage anger and choose to live a life free of the negative effects of this feeling. People who struggle to manage the anger should always seek assistance; because no one should have to live life at the mercy of an emotion that should ideally lead us to fight for what is right.

Chapter 3

Types of Anger

There are lots of different combinations of anger modes. No one experiences anger quite the same as any other person. You could be someone who screams and yells at someone who makes you angry but quickly forgives and forgets as soon as they've apologized.

You could be someone who keeps your anger bottled inside but secretly hopes that the person that made you angry receives karmic justice in the form of a terrible accident.

You could be a passive-aggressive person that chooses to direct your anger at the world as a whole, being sullen and uncooperative with everyone and everything.

While the specific experience of anger may be unique to each individual, some trends result in common types of anger. These will be addressed in the following list.

Even if the way that you experience anger isn't covered in this list, you will be able to see similarities in them that you can relate to, and in recognizing these similarities, you will be one step closer to identifying the anger management strategy that will work for you.

To make this list as accessible as possible, I will propose an example scenario and each anger type will be represented by a response to this situation typical of a person who possesses that type.

The scenario is simple: you have been turned down for a promotion in favor of someone with less experience and tenure in your company.

You have worked long and hard for this promotion, only to be denied it without explanation. You are angry, perhaps rightly so.

The question is, how do you express your anger?

Assertive Anger

What Does It Look Like?

If you possess assertive anger, in response to missing out on the promotion you will stop and ask yourself why you were turned down for the promotion and how you can improve to be considered next time.

You may even go so far as to approach your boss and ask for feedback to improve. This is the most constructive type of anger expression. Feelings of frustration and anguish are used as a catalyst for positive change. Anger is confronted, analyzed objectively, and acted upon with strategy and aforethought.

If you exhibit this type of anger, you can express it without causing damage or distress to those around you.

How Do I Control It?

Assertive anger is a type of controlled anger. It is defined as being in control as long as you are using it toward positive results such as overcoming fear, addressing injustice, or achieving the desired outcome.

Chronic Anger

What Does It Look Like?

If you possess chronic anger, in response to missing out on the promotion you will become resentful toward your boss, your job, your coworkers, and even toward your friends and family.

This type of anger is ongoing and is usually internalized but quick to make an appearance if you're provoked. It is a constant feeling of frustration; frustration with yourself, those around you, or your current circumstances. It can stem from a general feeling of not being in control of your situation, which leads to feelings of hopelessness that are expressed as perpetual irritability. This type of prolonged anger can impact your health and wellbeing negatively.

How Do I Control It?

You should stop and ask yourself what the cause of your anger is.

Once the cause of your anger has been identified, you should take steps to resolve the conflict, either inside yourself or in your current situation.

This may mean finding the strength to forgive whoever you feel has wronged you or communicating your feelings clearly and constructively to the party or parties responsible so that you can come to a mutual understanding.

Whichever positive avenue you choose to deal with your anger, dealing with it will allow you to let it go and prevent it from continuing to brew inside you.

Behavioral Anger

What Does It Look Like?

If you possess behavioral anger, in response to missing out on the promotion you will feel the need to react physically.

You may respond to the news by breaking something in the office, whether it be something small like a pencil or something large like a computer. You may feel the need to scrunch up a piece of paper and aggressively throw it into the wastebasket.

However, if you demonstrate an extreme type of behavioral anger, you may act aggressively toward your boss and/or coworkers. It's even possible for you to become violent toward these people.

Behavioral anger is a type of anger that causes you to lash out physically; to express your anger with physical, typically aggressive, actions. These actions can cause physical harm to those around you, but the volatile and uncontrolled nature of your behavior can negatively impact your ability to form lasting bonds with people, as it will cause people to distrust you.

How Do I Control It?

While a physical response to anger is quite often aggressive, it's important to note that anger doesn't automatically lead to aggression or violence.

Consider some self-reflection and try to figure out why you are choosing aggression as an outlet for your anger. If you are unable to do this, try to at least identify the warning signs of your aggressive behavior.

As soon as you feel yourself exhibiting these warning signs, try to step away from the situation that is causing the anger, or manage it by telling yourself to stay calm.

Say the words out loud and couple them with some of the deep breathing and muscle relaxation techniques that we will cover further in this book. If this fails and you still feel the need to express your anger physically, take up an active but constructive hobby like working out or running.

Verbal Anger

What Does It Look Like?

If you possess verbal anger, in response to missing out on the promotion you will seek to hurt your boss with words. You may shout at them, criticize them, ridicule them, whatever you think would hurt them the most.

You will also most likely turn on your savage tongue on the coworker that was promoted ahead of you as well as anyone else that gets in the way of your tirade.

Verbal anger is similar to behavioral anger in that the anger is expressed with acts of aggression that are intended to cause harm to whatever or whoever is making you angry. However, in the case of verbal anger, the harm inflicted is psychological, rather than physical.

How Do I Control It?

Breathe. Before saying anything, just breathe. The trick to controlling verbal anger is to delay your response long enough for you to prevent yourself from verbalizing your first though because that first thought is bound to be vicious.

The good thing about this type of anger is that your first reaction is verbal rather than physical, so you are already prone to expressing your anger with your words rather than your fists.

If you can stop yourself from vocalizing your first thought, you will be one step closer to being able to replace your tendency to resort to verbal abuse with a more constructive verbal expression of anger.

Judgmental Anger

What Does It Look Like?

If you possess judgmental anger, in response to missing out on the promotion you are likely to start bad-mouthing the parties involved and disparaging their worth. You might call your boss an idiot who doesn't know what they're doing.

You might say that the coworker that was promoted ahead of you is laughably unqualified for the position and that they won't last a week. You may say that the company you work for is beneath you and that you're better off working for a company that recognizes your talents.

Or you may say that the whole system is unfair and give up on any further opportunities to rise the ranks. Judgmental anger stems from a core belief that you are better than, or less than, others. It is usually the reaction of indignation to a perceived injustice or someone else's perceived shortcomings. The problem with judgmental anger is that no matter how justified your complaints maybe, they will only result in you pushing people away because you will constantly assume that the opinions of others are less valid than your own.

How Do I Control It?

The best way to manage judgmental anger is to exercise empathy and try to understand other people's viewpoints.

While you may disagree with someone's opinion, by trying to see things from their point of view, you are opening yourself up to other perspectives and potentially gaining insights that will give you more ideas on how to arrive at a positive solution.

If you can do this, you will get the bonus of people looking favorably upon you as you will have less of a tendency to come across as condescending or belittling.

Passive-Aggressive Anger

What Does It Look Like?

If you possess passive-aggressive anger, in response to missing out on the promotion you are likely to put less effort into your work going forward, procrastinating or delivering lack-luster results.

You may even become uncooperative at work, particularly when dealing with your boss or the coworker that was promoted ahead of you.

A passive-aggressive person tends to avoid expressing their anger outright and prefers to more subtle methods of venting such as non-compliance, sarcasm, or veiled mockery.

A passive-aggressive person will typically feel that this type of anger expression is less damaging than active-aggression. They may even not see their behavior as aggressive at all. However, people on the receiving end of passive-aggression usually notice the behavior change and this will cause feelings of confusion and frustration. Often, they will wish that the angry person would just confront them, rather than being passive-aggressive.

How Do I Control It?

The key to controlling passive-aggression is communication. Practice the assertive communication techniques that we will cover later in this book. Usually, passive-aggression is born from a fear of confrontation.

Try exploring this fear within yourself and little by little work on articulating your frustrations to your close friends and relatives.

Try analyzing the situation that is making you frustrated and using cognitive restructuring to come up with strategies for voicing your anger without damaging relationships.

With every successful exchange, you will see your confidence grow and your fear of confrontation melt away.

Overwhelmed Anger

What Does It Look Like?

If you possess overwhelmed anger, in response to missing out on the promotion you will not be able to control yourself.

You may break down and start crying. You may need to go somewhere private and scream your lungs out. You may need to rush to the bathroom to vomit.

Whatever form the response takes, it will be uncontrolled. Overwhelmed anger usually occurs when you feel that you don't have control over your situation or circumstances.

It is commonly experienced by people that have taken on more responsibility than they can handle or people that have been affected negatively by unexpected events. It occurs when a person feels more stress than their mind can handle.

Their mind is so full of negative thoughts that one additional trigger, even a small one, will result in a response that is strong and sudden.

How Do I Control It?

If you are experiencing overwhelmed anger you need to reach out for support. Find people to talk to, whether they are family members, friends, or coworkers.

You don't necessarily have to tell them how you're feeling, as long as you can ask them to provide you with some help and support to lighten your burden. Your life is probably so jam-packed with obligations that you can barely have time to yourself.

Balancing work, family, and a social life can be a nightmare and is bound to cause stress. By asking for help you can trim down the list of things to do, giving yourself more time and alleviating potential sources of stress.

Ask your partner to cook dinner every Wednesday night so that you can have one night a week away from the stove.

Ask your coworker to help you with your paperwork so that you take your time completing your other work.

Ask your best friend to babysit now and then so that you can have a night to yourself. Trim down your to-do list where you can and don't feel that you need to carry the entire weight of your world on your shoulders.

Self-Abusive Anger

What Does It Look Like?

If you possess self-abusive anger, in response to missing out on the promotion you will tell yourself that you didn't deserve the promotion and you were stupid to even have applied. You will swear at yourself and may even try to punish yourself with self-inflicted harm.

Self-abusive anger stems from feelings of humiliation, shame, and unworthiness. It is typically expressed internally with negative self-talk and self-harm.

Physical self-harm is particularly dangerous and can be represented in the form of self-inflicted wounds, drug use, alcoholism, or disordered eating.

Self-abusive anger has many similarities to clinical depression, though anger tends to spark action rather than inaction.

How Do I Control It?

The best way to manage self-abusive anger is to change the way you think. If your anger is self-abusive, it means you tend thoughts of self-defeat.

Exercising cognitive reframing techniques is a good way to transform these kinds of thoughts into more objective thoughts.

By learning to be objective, you will soon see that you are not always to blame, that other factors may be responsible for a situation that is causing you anguish.

Once you become better at being objective, you will be able to stop punishing yourself and think of more constructive ways to address the situation.

Retaliatory Anger

What Does It Look Like?

If you possess retaliatory anger, in response to missing out on the promotion you will become extremely defensive. You will attack your boss verbally and demand an explanation.

You will attack the coworker that was promoted ahead of you and list all the reasons why you are better suited for the position.

You may even quit your job. Retaliatory anger is an automatic and instinctive response to feelings of confrontation or aggression.

It is the need to fight back at those that have wronged you. In the case of the above scenario, you would feel that your professional abilities have been attacked and you will seek to defend these abilities while at the same time punishing those that have called them into question.

Retaliatory anger is the most common type of anger and while the resultant act of vengeance may not necessarily be deliberate, it often leads to escalation when retaliation is reciprocated in kind.

Chapter 4

Positive Thinking for Anger Free Life

We have seen how dealing with anger through avoidance is ineffective and why suppressing your anger can only lead to disaster. We explored the reasons why it is vital to manage anger with emotional intelligence and how we can cultivate it.

We are going to discuss the importance of cultivating positive thinking when dealing with anger problems.

Some of the important topics that we are going to tackle include how to change how we think, how to combat negative thoughts when they arise, and how to troubleshoot without anger.

We are also going to discuss how you can use relaxation and breathing to combat anger issues. Hopefully, you will have learned how to effectively deal with your anger in ways that are beneficial to yourself as well as the people in your life.

Change the Way You Think About Your Life

Whether you realize it or not, the way you think about yourself and your life greatly determines the quality of your life. If you constantly have happy and positive thoughts and feelings, life feels magical, exciting, and very fulfilling.

Pleasant thoughts and emotions can motivate you to take actions that improve your wellbeing and make your life more worthwhile.

You may decide to accept that job you have been hoping for or be jolted into action and open that business you've been thinking about.

On the other hand, if you are always plagued by negative thoughts, you may experience life as bleak, miserable, and dreadful.

You may find yourself withdrawn due to a fear of the world and the people in it, and you may lack the morale to make bold decisions and end up failing even at things that you are good at. Indeed, our thoughts are very reflective of our actions and can have a strong influence on the way our lives turn out to be. So, to improve the quality of our lives, we need first to change the way we think.

This, however, is easier said than done. It can be extremely difficult to be optimistic and positive when you constantly deal with anger issues.

Nevertheless, changing the way we think is fundamental if we hope to get rid of our chronic anger and begin living happily once more.

If you are wondering how you can reverse your negative thoughts and start thinking positively again, here are some of the tips which might help you overcome negative thinking.

Create Positive Affirmations

Most of us tend to make only negative affirmations as a way of dealing with our fear of disappointment. In a way, we hope that through being negative in the first place, we are preparing ourselves for scenarios where things don't work out in our favor.

If we expect to fail, we won't be too bothered when we do, right? In reality, this mindset only serves to hold us back since it diminishes our confidence in ourselves and keeps us from making bold decisions. Next time you feel like being negative, try motivating yourself with some positive self-talk instead.

Let Go of the Need be too Self-Critical

As humans, we tend towards being too hypercritical of ourselves. This is because we constantly compare ourselves with others.

We may feel like others are more advantaged than we are due to some superficial reason. Maybe we think they are too intelligent, too smart, too rich, or too talented.

This, however, is not always rooted in reality. In truth, all of us have our unique personalities with their advantages and setbacks. It is, therefore, very counterproductive for you to dwell on your deficiencies. If anything, you should use them as a motivation to grow and become better.

Appreciate Your Strengths

It is not uncommon for most people to take the things they have for granted. Many times, we complain about the things we don't have without appreciating what we do have.

For instance, instead of grumbling about the job that you failed to get, why don't you take the time to appreciate the fact that you are healthy enough to find another job? You'll be surprised at how this changes your outlook on life.

Don't Take Yourself Too Seriously

Many times, we find ourselves getting frustrated and anxious simply because we take ourselves too seriously.

We obsess over things because we think of life as some kind of competition which we have to win. This makes us anxious since we are afraid of failure.

By realizing that life is simply meant for living, we can relax and begin to enjoy ourselves instead of continually aggravating ourselves with worries and anxieties.

Like the great philosopher Alan Watts once said, "Man suffers because he takes too seriously that which the gods made for fun."

Strive to Live in the Present Moment

One of the reasons why many people struggle with anxiety and anger problems is because they simply worry too much about the past and the future.

We often tend to think that we will only be happy someday in the future when everything finally comes together in some ideal way.

The truth is that in doing so, we only postpone our happiness even as the clock of our mortality continues to tick.

It is far more beneficial and fulfilling to seek happiness in the present moment.

Take Care of Your Body

A healthy body is essential to creating happy thoughts. If your body is in distress, then you are more likely to become privy to negative self-talk and mental chatter. Ù

It is, therefore, essential to pay attention to your body's needs if you hope to improve the quality of your thoughts. The best part is that taking care of your body is not strenuous.

You simply have to practice eating healthily, engage in fitness exercises, and ensure you get enough sleep. Remember also to drink a lot of water and avoid drugs and alcohol.

When your body is adequately cared for and maintained, positive thinking naturally follows.

Focus on Yourself

It is very easy for us to see negativity and evil in other people and perceive ourselves as morally righteous. However, we all know that nobody is perfect, and everyone could use some self-improving.

So instead of constantly obsessing over the deficiencies of other people, you could turn the criticism inwards and focus on bettering those aspects of yourself, which you feel are deficient.

Have Faith in Yourself and Your Abilities

It is easy for us to lose confidence in ourselves when faced with the challenges of life. However, a lack of faith in ourselves can lead to feelings of inadequacy and victimhood, which leave us feeling powerless and resentful.

We need to cultivate self-confidence, even when we feel overwhelmed by life since this will provide us with the resilience to overcome any challenges that may beset us.

Think Differently and More Effectively When You Get Angry

Granted, feelings of anger and frustration can be very strong that they overwhelm us; it is essential to maintain a positive mindset when provoked.

Positive thinking can help us remove ourselves from the situation and evaluate it from a more objective point of view. As a result, we can be better placed to make rational choices and prevent our emotions from getting the better part of us.

Keeping a positive mindset when riled up, however, is not a very simple thing to do. The temptation to overreact can be too strong to resist when we feel seriously aggrieved by others.

Nevertheless, maintaining a positive mindset can help us deal more appropriately with our feelings of frustration without causing harm to ourselves and other people.

While you may be justifiably angry at someone for something they may have done, you need to try and keep your thinking unclouded, since this will help you make better decisions.

Here are some of the tips which can help you think differently and more effectively when you get angry:

Identify the Cause of Your Anger

Many times, we end up erupting in aggression when angry simply because we do not understand the real cause of the anger.

Frustration without apparent reason typically leads to more frustration, which can easily lead to explosive altercations when the final straw breaks. To change how you think about your anger, therefore, you need to narrow down on the real cause as soon as you feel the symptoms in your body.

This will not only prevent you from overreacting, but it will also stop you from making wrong judgments like blaming someone unfairly.

Take Yourself out of the Situation

It is very difficult to think clearly when you are smack in the middle of a situation, which triggered your anger in the first place.

To be able to resolve the problem, you need to remove yourself from your situation so that you can collect your thoughts and gain clarity. You may want to take a walk or go into your room for a few minutes.

Alternatively, read your favorite book or take your pet for a walk until you feel calm. Once the tension dissipates, you will be thinking much more clearly and thus be more capable of dealing with the problem.

Realize that you are Choosing your Response

Often, when people get provoked and react in violent ways, which gets them in trouble, they like to plead defense by saying their anger made them do it.

However, while anger can make you feel very strong emotions, ultimately, the choice on how to respond rests firmly with you.

So, before you make any rash decisions out of anger, which you may later end up regretting, you need to remind yourself that you are the one choosing how to respond. By taking responsibility for your anger in this way, you can start thinking more effectively and seek out healthy solutions for dealing with your rage.

Remember that Your Beliefs do not Necessarily Reflect Reality

It is very common for people to shift the responsibility of their anger on others instead of taking it upon themselves.

Whenever we get angry, we tend to always see others as toxic and ourselves as saintly, which only works out against us in the end.

The truth of the matter, however, is that we, ourselves, can be very toxic to ourselves as well as to other people. We may be disposing ourselves to anger by imposing our worldview and values onto others or expecting them to meet our unrealistic expectations. It is, therefore, important to remind yourself that your beliefs about what or who made you angry may not be grounded in reality.

Subjecting yourself to this criticism when angry can help you attain a realistic perspective on your anger.

Respond Instead of Reacting

It can be very difficult to maintain a cool demeanor and engage in mature discourse when fired up with rage.

Most times, when we engage in a discussion when we are angry, we are seeking validation for our hurt feelings.

We may, therefore, be more inclined to interrupt the other person, yell at them, or completely dismiss everything they say. However, this is not in any way helpful when it comes to dealing with anger.

To think more clearly and effectively about our anger, we need to listen to the other person intently and respond tactfully with clear and concise sentences. This can help us begin thinking effectively when dealing with our feelings of frustration.

Troubleshooting Without Anger

Throughout this book, we have reiterated the primacy of anger as a human emotion, as well as the role it plays in our lives.

We found out that anger can help us tackle problems of injustice that threaten the very fabric of our society. So then, dear, you probably agree that anger has a special role to play in our lives.

Nevertheless, unrestrained anger can be detrimental to the achievement of our objectives and aims.

Whether it's in our relationships with our loved ones or our professional careers, unmanaged anger can hinder progress and success.

For this reason, we must find a way of solving problems that make us angry without letting our feelings control us.

While anger can motivate us to tackle the problems we face and make our situations better, chronic anger serves no purpose other than drain useful energy, which could be channeled to more productive activities.

It is, therefore, important that our anger is managed in healthy ways and expressed in creative endeavors. Instead of using anger to destroy and tear-down ourselves and each other, we should strive to use it for the benefit of ourselves and others.

Chapter 5

How is anger treated?

There are several techniques with which it is possible to manage anger, let's see them in detail.

Visualization

This technique involves your imagination. You have to visualize yourself keeping calm amidst the anger of another person.

See yourself calm and collected, while the other person is throwing invectives at you. Picture yourself remaining calm despite the embarrassment caused by a colleague.

If you have certain events or incidents in the past that made you angry, imagine those incidents and visualize yourself acting calmly in such situations.

Your visualization must be vivid; include your facial expressions and every detail of the behavior that you would want to do.

Reflexology/Acupressure

Massaging or pressing certain trigger spots in your body can relieve pain, decrease anxiety/depression and ease anger. In the case of anger, the middle finger is involved.

All you have to do is to massage or press the length of the middle finger of your right hand for 3 to 5 minutes. Switch to your left hand and do the same. While doing these, inhale and exhale deeply.

Continue the action until your anger has subsided.

Progressive Muscle Relaxation

Again, this technique helps manage anger by relieving stress and tension in the body. It also works if you have a nagging pain or ache whenever you feel stressed.

Muscle tension is a response the body gives whenever you are stressed and tense. This could result in feelings of anger. So, progressive muscle relaxation helps relieve muscle tension to prevent anger.

You may start with the use of an audio recording to aid your memorization of the muscle groups. Once you know the muscle groups, you can do everything on your own. The best thing

Mindfulness Meditation

Mindfulness meditation is a kind of meditation that has been proven by several studies to be of immense benefit to the mind and the body.

It is a kind of mental training that teaches you self-awareness by focusing your mind on your experiences, emotions, thoughts, and sensations in the present.

Mindfulness practice may combine breathing exercises with visualization, imagery, and muscle relaxation.

This particular meditation helps very much with anger management because it trains you to become aware of your emotions, including anger before they jump on you.

It also teaches you to focus on the present without giving any thought to the past or the future and also to accept everything without judgment.

To engage in mindfulness meditation, here are the steps you can follow

Get a quiet, comfortable, and noiseless place for practice. You can either use a chair or sit on the floor. Wherever you decide to sit, ensure you sit in an upright position with your back straight but not stiff.

Clear your mind of all thoughts of the past or future while immersing yourself completely in the present. Stay grounded in the present. Draw your awareness to the rise and fall of your breath, observing the sensation that the air moving in and out produces in your body as you breathe.

Focus on the rise and fall of your belly and the in and out of the air in your nostrils and the mouth. Pay mind to the change in rhythm as you inhale and exhale.

Become aware of your thoughts as they come and go. Do not judge whatever it thought is, be it fear, worry, frustration, anxiety, or anything. Just observe as the thoughts float around in your mind.

Note that you shouldn't try to suppress the thoughts or ignore them. Simply make a mental note of them while focusing on your breathing.

If you notice yourself getting carried away in the thoughts, don't judge yourself. Simply return your mind to your breathing after taking note of the thoughts. Don't be harsh with yourself.

Once you are nearing the end of your meditation session, stay seated for one or two minutes and gradually become aware of your immediate environment. Appreciate the surrounding for a while and then slowly get up. Go about your day with your mind at rest.

In practicing mindfulness meditation, you can also incorporate it into other activities like doing the dishes, driving, exercising, or even brushing your teeth. Mindfulness is best practiced right before you go to sleep or when you just wake up.

Sound therapy

Natural sounds can be calming and therapeutic. All you have to do is to listen to the sounds of nature and they would appease you.

Lie or sit down comfortably in a place where you won't be disturbed. Listen to the sounds of the falling rain, the blowing wind, the wooing sound of the waves, the chirping of birds, the waterfalls, and similar sounds of nature. Some people prefer soft music of their favorite songs. It doesn't matter what sound you choose, provided that it calms you.

Hypnosis

Hypnosis by a certified expert can help you manage your anger, anxiety, and stress. Nevertheless, this is not recommended for persons, who have psychiatric problems. It may aggravate their condition. Also, ensure that the person performing the procedure is licensed and legitimate.

Autosuggestion

In this method, you repeatedly suggest to yourself the positive behaviors that you want to acquire. It's like hypnotizing yourself until the thoughts penetrate your subconscious and consequently, change the way you behave. This should be done at least daily. You can do it several times a day as well.

Psychologist/Psychiatrist

This is your last alternative when nothing could work for you. You need the help of a licensed expert, who will guide you in managing your anger, stress, and anxiety. Your psychologist will assist you in recognizing positive behaviors, and the advantage of choosing them over the negatives.

Chapter 6

Understanding Mental Health and Anger

Even though no succinct definition exists, mental health is essentially your frame of mind and way to deal with life. Mental, environmental, hereditary, or physiological variables profoundly affected by and large mental advancement.

What is mental illness? Mental illness weakens your capacity to perform routine assignments, cultivate healthy connections, or adapt to anger or stress. It might range from outrageous emotional episodes, silly or destructive ideas, and social problems.

How important is mental health? Your mental health hugely affects each part of your life.

Education

Persons with mental problems socially seclude themselves and create anxiety issues and fixation problems. Great mental health guarantees an inside and out instructive experience that improves social and scholarly abilities that lead to self-assurance and better evaluations.

Relationships

Mental health to a great extent adds to the working of human connections. Mental illness can hamper even fundamental connections with family, companions, and associates.

Many people experiencing mental illness think that it's difficult to support connections, have problems with responsibility or closeness, and much of the time, experience sexual health issues.

Sleep

Powerlessness to deal with stress or anxiety can cause a sleeping disorder. Regardless of whether you manage to nod off, you may awaken twelve times during the night with considerations of what turned out badly the previous day or how awful tomorrow will be.

You may create serious sleeping issues that leave you depleted and less productive.

Physical health

Your mental state straightforwardly influences your body. For instance, stress can lead to hypertension or stomach ulcers. Mentally healthy people are at a lower hazard for some health issues.

Anger and Mental Health

Anger is most closely connected with anxiety. People who have anger management problems are frequently profoundly on edge and stressed.

They are regularly exceptionally working people who expect a lot from themselves and a lot from those whom they encircle themselves with.

Anger management problems are a characteristic side-effect of their life. A lot of these people have exceptionally significant levels of either generalized anxiety or social anxiety.

These two sorts of anxiety are adding to their anger management problems. It's a lot simpler for these people, typically men, to state that, "I have anger management problems," than to state that, "I experience the ill effects of social or generalized anxiety."

People with social anxiety think that it's difficult to be out in the open spots, for instance, malls, where there will be a lot of others around and where a simple exit isn't constantly present.

For instance, in a train when riding between home and work, when the train is moving, they are not ready to leave the train until the following stop. People with generalized anxiety have low strength in stressful situations in their life.

Some portion of their on-edge response to these situations is to become angry. Another mental condition related to anger is depression. A few specialists accept that depression will influence 1 out of 5 people, at any one point in time. 80% of people will endure depression at one point in their life.

So, it is an extremely, normal mental health condition. Depression can be a very baffling condition to have because there is no obvious solution to it. This is particularly disappointing for goal-driven people who frequently experience the ill effects of anger problems in any case.

There's no solution to it. No obvious solution to it. They can't go for a run or drink some lager, drink some alcohol, or eat some nourishment or converse with somebody about it.

Depression is a lot more perplexing than that. A typical response to depression and anger is to take the disappointment out on others. Once more, it's important that people see the truth about depression, and get it evaluated and treated.

Anger Management Is an Inability to Handle Negative Emotions

Recollect your life now. What do you do at whatever point you have a negative emotion? For instance, when you are down or on edge or stressed what do you do?

Do you sit alone unobtrusively and deal with it time permitting? Or then again do you attempt to dispose of it through alcohol, work out, Facebook, Twitter, Twitter, drugs, smoking, conversing with companions or family?

The vast majority will do the last mentioned because we've never been instructed how to deal with our negative emotions.

Lamentably for a great many people, our emotions resemble an exciting ride. It goes up when we have strong, positive emotions. It levels when we have unbiased emotions. It plunges when we have negative emotions for a specific timeframe, and afterward the cycle proceeds.

Tips on How to Improve Your Emotional and Mental Health

Your present lifestyle may not be advantageous in keeping up your emotional and mental health. Our general public is overworked, overstressed, and excessively centered around things that don't bolster great psychological prosperity.

Being proactive and doing things that cultivate great mental health can be a ground-breaking approach to enhance the nature of your day-to-day life.

Apply these tips regularly: Cooperate with others. Having positive and healthy associations with others has an important impact on psychological health. Cooperating and associating with others will prevent you from feeling forlorn.

If you disconnect yourself, don't get out of the house other than work, and run tasks, you rapidly can turn out to be desolate and start feeling discouraged. Rather find something to do that gets you out of the house and around people.

Keep your body healthy. Poor physical health can result in difficulties with mental health. The better you feel physically, the better you'll feel psychological, as well.

Make it a propensity for consistently practicing and it doesn't need to be in a rec center, you can take a run or walk your dog.

Swimming is additionally a decent exercise technique. Whatever it is that gets your body going and gets your pulse up. Practicing discharges endorphins and endorphins make you feel great, loose, and calm.

Build up a goal and endeavor to meet it. There will most certainly be some stress and challenges along the way, yet it will be well justified, despite all the trouble once you achieved those. Learn how to deal with stress viably. A large portion of us makes them calm propensities that may appear to be viable yet as a general rule neglect to address the reason for stress. A few of us deal with stress in ways that make the situation more awful.

In case you're monetarily stressed, eating a tub of frozen yogurt will at present leave you broke, yet you'll likewise wind up putting on weight. Look for positive solutions.

Exercises, for example, working out, investing energy with a friend, or perusing a book can be healthy alternatives for bringing down your stress.

Make time for yourself where you can loosen up and unwind.

Stressing over something you have no control over isn't healthy and doesn't help in settling the problem or issue. Ù

For instance, if you have cash issues and your stress and stress over it, it won't take care of the problem, it's just a motivation for you to stress out considerably more.

Rather take a full breath and think of an arrangement to diminish your costs in specific zones to have cash for progressively important things.

Invest energy every day on an agreeable action. It could be taking your dog for a walk, going for a run, going out to see a movie, get a back rub, or in any event, playing with your children.

It doesn't matter what it is you do, as long as you appreciate doing it and focus on things other than work or things you have to complete or take care of. Make space for a bit of "personal time."

Practice the specialty of forgiveness. Anger and hard feelings achieve close to nothing. They put you in a horrendous mental cycle that corrupts your sense of prosperity.

Consistently you're angry or upset the second you're troubled. Accept things as lessons learned and proceed onward as opposed to harping on the things that occurred before. Give your time to other people. Helping somebody in need is a great method to support how you feel about yourself. It's additionally a great method to meet others that are likewise thoughtful and giving.

Consider a gathering of people you'd prefer to help and find an association that helps them. It could likewise be a friend, coworker, or somebody you just met, if they are in urgent need, give them a hand, and regardless of whether it's simply discussing with them, some simply need somebody that tunes in and cares.

Learn how to quiet your mind. Your mind seldom gets a rest, not even while you're sleeping. Throughout the night, you're likely hurling, turning, and dreaming.

There are numerous ways to rest your mind: asking, contemplating, and rehearsing mindfulness are only a couple.

Our brains are restless. They're continually thinking, foreseeing, and recalling. Regardless of whether you don't see that you are contemplating something, your subliminal mind thinks constantly.

Learn how to control yours. Meditation can assist you with learning how to quiet down your mind. It might take a couple of attempts because our minds continue straying and don't have any desire to be quiet; however, with practice, you'll arrive.

Request help. If you break your arm, you look for medicinal help. In case you're having a psycho-intelligent issue, there's no explanation not to do likewise.

Regardless of what your challenge might be, there's somebody accessible with the skill to help.

You don't need to see an advocate or advisor if you don't have any desire to; you could essentially go to your family or friends, even a minister or anybody eager to tune in and to give you some assistance. Sometimes we can't do everything all alone. Requesting help isn't a shortcoming, rather, it shows quality since you recognize that you can't do it all alone and you demonstrate solidarity to connect with somebody who can support you.

Keep a journal. Writing down your considerations on paper following a long, hard day is restorative. It discharges pressure and can give you an alternate point of view.

When writing in a journal, you can be as obtuse and legit as you need without stressing over upsetting anybody with what you state since it is for your eyes as it were. It resembles a punching pack, on terrible days you can let out the entirety of your anger and dissatisfaction, and on great days you can share your fervor and fun things which will be great recollections and great jolts of energy when you have an awful day.

Emotional and mental health are both basic to your general prosperity. At the point when any segment of your health is enduring, it turns out to be substantially more testing to be a viable parent, life partner, friend, or representative.

All parts of your life, particularly your physical health, can endure. Utilize these tips to address your psychological health. In case you're not feeling better, it's time to look for help.

Chapter 7

Understanding & Handling Anger in Relationships

In this chapter, you'll discover how anger follows a predictable cycle in romantic relationships, and how you can keep it from driving you and your partner apart.

You'll learn some key communication skills that will empower you both. Most of the techniques and ideas in this section also apply to handling problems in family relationships and friendships.

The Cycle of Anger in Relationships

Angry people often have angry relationships. Usually, one person feels mistreated or frustrated, which kick starts a destructive cycle that drags both partners down.

The cycle normally goes like this:

- Partner A becomes angry because they believe that Partner B has treated them badly.

This mistreatment—which can be actual or perceived—could be trivial or major. For example, Partner A might believe that Partner B has been flirting with someone at work and feel angry as a result.

- Partner A engages in negative, destructive behaviors.

Because Partner A doesn't know how to handle their own emotions or start a calm conversation with their partner, they resort to destructive behavior instead. They may use overt forms of aggression, such as shouting or passive-aggressive tactics like sulking.

- Partner B notices Partner A's behaviors.

Unless they are willfully oblivious, Partner B will pick up on Partner A's anger. Partner B will feel attacked, blamed, and possibly rejected.

- Partner B becomes angry at Partner A.

If they don't have the skills to start a constructive dialogue with Partner A, Partner B responds with their anger.

The cycle continues. Over time, both partners may slip into a state of habitual anger. The underlying issues are never resolved. One or both partners might lash out, but neither knows how to reach a mutual understanding.

If this cycle continues long enough, both people can become resentful of one another. They may start believing that their relationship is doomed. They stop enjoying one another's company and may split up.

Sometimes this is the best solution; not all relationships are destined to work out. However, many relationships could be saved if both partners take the time to master basic communication skills and simple anger management techniques.

Exercise: The Anger Cycle in Your Relationship

Think back to the last time you felt angry at your partner. How did both of you move through the anger cycle? What happened to make you or your partner so angry? Did you manage to resolve the issue, or is it still causing problems in your relationship?

How to Shut the Cycle Down Before It Begins

The good news is that the cycle isn't inevitable. If you learn how to communicate your wants and needs in a relationship and address problems as they arise, you can enjoy a more harmonious life together.

Try these strategies:

1. Reframe your partner's behavior

Suppose your partner promised to cook dinner one evening. You come home from work and find your partner watching TV instead, with no sign that they are even thinking about making a meal. How would you respond? You could berate them for being lazy. Or you could take a passive-aggressive approach, perhaps by ignoring them and sighing as you start making your dinner. Both responses would let them know you are disappointed and angry.

Alternatively, you could try a different tactic and reframe the situation. You could ask, "What would be a more charitable interpretation of their behavior here?" In this instance, you might say to yourself, "There's no evidence that they've forgotten completely. They might have lost track of the time, or maybe they were waiting until I got home so we could talk for a while before they start cooking."

How do you think you'd speak and act towards your partner if you chose to reframe their behavior like this? You'd probably be more patient, ask straightforward questions instead of berating them, and focus on the facts rather than starting a fight.

[Of course, some behaviors can't and shouldn't be reframed. If your partner is behaving in an abusive way, it's not helpful or safe to reframe their actions. Focus on keeping yourself safe instead.]

2. Distance yourself from the situation

In the last chapter, you learned about self-distancing. Take a step back and imagine that one of your friends or relatives were in your situation.

Watch the scenario play out as though it were happening to someone else instead. What would you advise them to do?

3. Use constructive communication to resolve your differences instead of just expressing anger

This is the most important step. The best way to break the anger cycle is to start a mature, mutually beneficial conversation with your partner. Respectful conversations:

- Give all parties the chance to make their views known

- Are honest
- Come from a place of mutual compassion
- Are never abusive
- Can be difficult and draining, but allow both sides to work towards a solution

Here are a few things to keep in mind:

1. Using insults and generalizations only makes things worse

Insulting someone puts them on the defensive. If your partner insults you, don't pay them back in kind. It's better to walk away completely than let yourself be drawn into a mud-slinging match.

2. Shouting is never helpful

Shouting can feel cathartic, but it escalates the conflict. It invites hostility and keeps your body in a state of high alert. Your partner will probably shout back, and both of you will feel worse.

3. Seeking to understand, rather than persuade, is the best tactic

Are you more concerned with winning, or do you want to reach an understanding? If you treat every conversation like a battleground, your partner will soon realize that you don't want to work with them - you only want to be right.

Put your ego to one side and concentrate on gathering information. Don't minimize your partner's feelings by telling them to "calm down," and don't imply they are overreacting.

4. Planning for difficult conversations is a smart idea

It's OK to plan a conversation. It might seem strange, but writing down the points you want to cover and even rehearsing how you will explain your point of view can be very helpful.

Exercise: Planning for a Sensitive Conversation

Are there any ongoing problems in your relationship? If you and your partner keep arguing about the same "hot button" topic over and over again, it's time to try a new approach. Instead of waiting for the subject to come up in conversation and then repeating your usual points, make some notes on how the issue makes you feel, what you'd like you and your partner to do differently, and a few ideas on how the two of you could work together to come up with solutions to your problems.

Ask your partner when the two of you can discuss the issue. Using notes will help you structure the conversation and prevent you from getting overwhelmed.

5. Giving each other time to talk, checking your understanding, then swapping roles lets you both feel heard

Decide who will speak first. Flip a coin if you can't decide. Set a timer for 3-5 minutes. The first speaker gets to talk, uninterrupted, while the timer is running.

The listener's job is to do whatever it takes to keep themself from butting in while trying to understand what their partner is saying.

When the speaker has finished, the listener paraphrases the main points to check that they've understood what was said. The partners then swap roles.

Only after each person has had a chance to express their views do they work together to solve their problems. Trying to jump straight to the problem-solving stage won't work.

If you interrupt your partner when it's their turn to talk, apologize immediately and ask them to keep going. If your partner interrupts you when it's your turn to speak, pause the timer, calmly wait until they have finished, then say, "I'm going to talk again now.

Please don't interrupt until the time is up." If they can't respect this boundary, take a time out and resume the conversation later.

6. Use "I" statements when talking about your feelings

"I" statements are less confrontational than sentences that begin with "You," which often come across as aggressive or judgmental. Avoid starting sentences with "You always," "You never," or "You should."

Instead, begin with a statement about the other person's behavior, then follow up by explaining how it makes you feel.

For example, instead of saying, "You never do your share of the housework!" it would be more constructive to say, "When you leave your dirty dishes in the sink every day for me to clean, I feel unappreciated."

Next, spell out what you want from the other person. Keep your requests reasonable and specific. To continue with the example above, you could say, "I would like you to clean up every other day because this means we are splitting the job equally."

7. Notice patterns

Good communication depends on both parties being willing to put in the necessary effort. If your partner doesn't want to cooperate, don't drive yourself crazy by holding onto the hope that their communication skills will improve.

In some cases, you might even need to think about whether you want to continue with the relationship.

For example, if you've been trying all the techniques in this chapter for several weeks, yet your partner seems uninterested in understanding your feelings or making positive changes, you need to realize that your wellbeing just isn't as important to them as theirs is to you.

8. Don't make unfounded accusations

Before accusing your partner of doing something wrong, stop for a moment and ask yourself whether your suspicions are supported by evidence. A gut feeling or hunch doesn't count.

9. Don't drag up the past

Unless it's directly relevant to whatever problems you're having in the present, leave the past where it belongs.

Many couples get drawn into discussions and arguments about people and events that have no bearing on their current problems, which only makes it harder to tackle issues that affect them in the present.

10. Don't use sarcasm

Sarcasm is a form of mockery, and mockery has no place in respectful conversations. It achieves nothing, aside from aggravating your partner. If you catch yourself making a sarcastic remark, apologize immediately.

11. Watch your body language

Check that your words, tone of voice, and body language are in alignment. Keep your tone of voice steady, keep your arms and legs uncrossed, and avoid staring or using another hostile body language.

12. Don't stonewall

Psychologist and relationship expert John Gottman has identified four signs that a relationship is in trouble: criticism, contempt, defensiveness, and stonewalling.

To stonewall, someone means to withdraw or shut down when they are trying to talk to you, and it isn't a healthy response to conflict. Calling a timeout is a good idea if an argument is spiraling out of control or you aren't making any progress, but don't withdraw completely.

Chapter 8

Triumph Over Anger and Depression

Anger usually occurs as a natural response to feeling attacked, frustrated, or even being humiliated. It is human nature to get angry.

The fury, therefore, is not a bad feeling per se, because, at times, it can prove to be very useful. How is this even possible?

Anger can open one's mind and help them identify their problems, which could drive one to get motivated to make a change, which could help in molding their lives.

When is Anger a Problem?

Anger, as we have just seen, is normal in life. The problem only comes in when one cannot manage their anger, and it causes harm to people around them or even themselves.

How does one notice when their anger is becoming harmful? When one starts expressing anger through unhelpful or destructive behavior, or even when one's mental and physical health starts deteriorating. That's when one knows that the situation is getting out of hand.

It is the way a person behaves that determines whether or not they have problems with their anger. If the way they act affects their life or relationships, then there is a problem, and they should think about getting some support or treatment.

What is Unhelpful Angry Behavior?

Anger may be familiar to everyone, but people usually express their rage in entirely different ways. How one behaves when they are angry depends on how much control they have over their feelings.

People who have less control over their emotions tend to have some unhelpful angry behaviors.

These are behaviors that cause damage to themselves or even damage to people or things around them.

They include:

- **Inward Aggression.** This is where one directs their anger towards themselves. Some of the behaviors here may include telling oneself that they hate themselves, denying themselves, or even cutting themselves off the world.
- **Non-Violent or Passive Aggression.** In this case, one does not direct their anger anywhere; rather, they stick with the feeling in them. Some of the behaviors here may include ignoring people, refusing to speak to people, refusing to do tasks, or even deliberately doing chores poorly or late. These types of behaviors are usually the worst ways to approach such situations. They may seem less destructive and harmful, but they do not relieve one of the heavy burdens that are causing them to be angry.

Weigh Your Options

In life, many things may be out of one's control. These things vary from the weather, the past, other people, intrusive thoughts, physical sensations, and one's own emotions.

Despite all these, the power to choose is always disposable to any human. Even though one might not be able to control the weather, one can decide whether or not to wear heavy clothing. One can also choose how to respond to other people.

The first step, therefore, in dealing with anger is to recognize a choice.

Steps to Take in Managing Anger

A "Should" Rule is Broken. Everybody has some rules and expectations for one's behavior, and also for other people's behavior. Some of these rules include, "I should be able to do this,"

"She should not treat me like this," and, "They should stay out of my way." Unfortunately, no one has control over someone else's actions.

Therefore, these rules are always bound to be broken, and people may get in one's way. This can result in anger, guilt, and pressure.

It is, therefore, essential to first break these "should" rules to fight this anger. The first step to make in breaking these rules is to accept the reality of life that someone usually has very little control over other people's lives.

The next step is for one to choose a direction based on one's values. How does one know their values? One can identify their values by what angers them, frustrates them, or even enrages them.

For example, let's take the rule of "They should stay out of my way." This rule may mean the values of communication, progress, or even cooperation. What do these values mean to someone? Does one have control over them?

Finally, one can act by their values. To help with this, here are two questions one should ask themselves:

- What does one want in the long run?
- What constructive steps can one take in that direction?
- What Hurts?

The second step is to find the real cause of pain or fear after breaking the rules. These rules usually do not mean the same as one's body. This is because some states of being can hurt one's self-esteem more than others.

To understand this better, let's take the example of Susan, who expects that no one should talk ill of her. Then suddenly John comes up to her and says all manner of things to her. This, therefore, makes Susan enraged. In such a scenario, Susan should ask herself what hurts her. The answer to this question will bring out a general belief about John and herself.

She will think that "John is rude," "She is powerless," or even that "She is being made the victim." All these thoughts may hurt her.

What may even hurt her most is that she has no control over John's behavior.

Once she has noted that she has no control, she may now consider seeing John's words as a mere opinion rather than an insult. This will make her not see herself as a victim, but as a person just receiving a piece of someone else's mind about herself.

Hot Thoughts

After one has identified what hurts them, it is now time to identify and, most importantly, replace the hot, anger-driven, and reactive thoughts with more level-headed, more relaxed, and reflective thoughts. Here are some fresh ideas that may be of importance to someone:

- Hot thought: "How mean can he be!"
- A cool thought: "He thinks he is so caring."
- Hot thought: "They are stupid!"
- A cool thought: "They are just human."

Anger

All the above steps, as one may have noticed, relate to the thoughts. This is because one has first to tackle the ideas before now getting to the emotion.

In this step, therefore, one is going to respond to the anger arousal itself. There are three ways that one can follow to respond to this emotion:

One may indulge in relaxation. This relaxation can come in many forms, like enjoying some music, practicing some progressive muscle relaxation like yoga, and also visualization.

One may also use that feeling to do some constructive work. When one is angry, there is usually a large amount of energy that one uses at that time.

This is the reason that when angry, one can break down things that they would never break when calm. Imagine, therefore, how much that energy would do for someone if just directed to some constructive work.

One may also try to redefine anger when one gets angry. What does this mean? Once a person is angry, one can try to remind themselves of how anger is a problem that fuels aggression and can cause harm to loved ones and even oneself.

Moral Disengagement

In simple words, this step will help one examine the beliefs that turn anger into aggression. These beliefs usually act as mere excuses or justification for destructive acts.

Some of these beliefs include "I don't care," "This is the only way I can get my point across," or even "It is high time they recognize me." These beliefs need to be identified early enough and gotten rid of before they can con one into throwing one's morals aside.

One sure way of getting rid of them is by reminding oneself of the cost of such beliefs and the advantages of striving for understanding.

Aggression

In this step, one now needs to examine the behaviors that arise from aggression and try to fight them. Fighting these behaviors can be achieved if one calms down and puts themselves in the other person's shoes. This will help one understand why the other person is acting in such a manner, what they may be feeling, or even what they may be thinking. This approach will help to decrease the anger for all parties involved.

Increase the chance of having a reasonable conversation with the parties involved, and thus everybody is heard.

Conclusion

It is unthinkable for somebody to never get irate. Things dependably happen in our lives that make us furious and need to lash out. Nobody is impeccable and it is alright to show feeling and get upset. Be that as it may, a few individuals can't control their anger and they get way out of line.

An answer for them is to take anger management courses to remain calm and to express it more suitably and respectably.

At the point when anger is bungled, it can make many issues for the individual who is agitated as well as particularly for people around them.

Residential misuse is a colossal issue for somebody who can't control their anger. A man or lady may need to lash out at their mate on the off chance that they are furious and this makes a lot of issues in their marriage and even with their kids.

Individuals who have gone to anger management courses figure out how to channel that anger so it's not damaging.

Street wrath is another issue brought on by blundered anger. Individuals will get past irate on the off chance that somebody cuts them off.

In compelling instances of street fury, individuals have been shot or gravely harmed. Separation is a typical issue when a mate has an anger management issue.

Nobody needs to associate with a man who is constantly furious and can't remain calm. As much as a man may adore another, there is continually something that they can't endure. It can be truly hard to watch adoration blur away in face of an issue with anger.

To maintain a strategic distance from any of these circumstances, numerous individuals are thinking that it was supportive to search out proficient help. One of the best streets for this is anger management courses. It is not something to be humiliated of on the off chance that you need help remaining calm.

If you are reluctant about seeing somebody eye to eye you can simply discover help on the web. Notwithstanding anger management classes, you can likewise use things like sound tapes and books to cause figure out how to move the negative sentiments into more positive ones.

Being frantic doesn't need to result in fierce conduct or undue anxiety. One of the things that a great many people with anger issues don't understand is how their upheavals influence other individuals.

When they get some direction in how to deal with their anger, they can start to perceive how much quieter and more content everybody around them is, the point at which they aren't shouting and shouting because something didn't go an incredible way they needed.

There is no utilization in packaging antagonistic emotions any longer. It does not just harm you and the individuals around you that you think about the most, yet it likewise isn't solid.

Anger management courses will help you feel a ton better and truly begin getting a charge out of a more satisfied, all the more satisfying life.

Do you ever get irate in trivial circumstances? What circumstances are these? It is safe to say that you are ready to control your anger soon? The responses to every one of these inquiries would let you know a ton about the sort of identity you have.

Anger management assumes the main part in identity improvement. Most men and ladies think that it was exceptionally hard to manage anger and wind-up having circumstances out of extents. This additionally turns into an identity obstacle as a part of their identity improvement furthermore causes different wellbeing issues. Anger is likewise considered as one of the greatest foes of a human body and soul. It weakens judgment, can make a man rough and the individual can even lose his/her connections.

Along these lines, it is critical to figure out how to control anger or, maybe, to figure out how to channelize it in such a route, to the point that it might be useful.

Numerous advantages you can pick up from having the capacity to deal with your anger.

One may never comprehend the blissful advantages of anger management classes unless they encounter it and see an identity change as a part of their identity.

CPSIA information can be obtained
at www.ICGtesting.com
Printed in the USA
BVHW081657260221
601199BV00009B/988